THE RUBAIYAT OF OMAR KHAYYAM

THE RUBAIYAT OF OMAR KHAYYAM

By

JOHN MILTON HAY

GYAN

Published by

Gyan Publishing House
5, Ansari Road
Daryaganj, New Delhi-110002
Phone: 011-47034999, 9811692060
E-mail: books@gyanbooks.com

Distribution Network
gyanbooks.com
India, USA, Canada, UK, Australia, France

ISBN : 978-81-212-6232-3 (PB)
First Published, 1918

2nd Impression 2022

Printed at: Gyan Press, Delhi.

The
Rubaiyat of Omar Khayyam
Author: John Milton Hay

The Rubaiyat of Omar Khayyam

THE RUBAIYAT

DWELL here three sad sweet spirits: Perfume
born
Of fading Rose-leaves, visions of The Thorn
Behind each Flower of Joy in Life's Bouquet,
And one long Sigh we make too oft to scorn.

A HAIR perhaps divides the False and
True;"
Or False or True thy Verses, we this due
Of meed bestow on One most bitter-sweet:
We read and dream, then dream and read anew.

CHARLES P. NETTLETON.

ADDRESS OF JOHN HAY

OMAR KHAYYAM

By HON. JOHN HAY

ADDRESS DELIVERED DECEMBER 8, 1897, AT THE DINNER OF THE OMAR KHAYYAM CLUB, LONDON.

I CAN never forget my emotions when I first saw FitzGerald's translations of the Quatrains. Keats, in his sublime ode on Chapman's Homer has described the sensation once for all:

> Then felt I like some watcher of the skies
> When a new planet swims into his ken.

The exquisite beauty, the faultless form, the singular grace of those amazing stanzas were not more wonderful than the depth and breadth of their profound philosophy, their knowledge of life, their dauntless courage, their serene facing of the ultimate problems of life and death. Of course the doubt did not spare me, which has assailed many as ignorant as I was of the literature of the East, whether it was the poet or the translator to whom was due this splendid result. Was it, in fact, a reproduction of an antique song, or the mystification of a great modern, careless of fame and scornful of his time? Could it be possible that in the Eleventh Century, so far away as Khorassan, so accomplished a man of letters lived, with such distinction, such breadth, such insight, such calm disillusions, such cheerful and jocund despair? Was this "Weltschmerz," which we thought a malady of our day, endemic in Persia in 1100? My doubt only lasted till I came upon a literal translation of the *Rubaiyat*, and I saw that not the least remarkable quality of FitzGerald's poem was its fidelity to the original. ¶ In short, Omar was a FitzGerald, or FitzGerald was a reincarnation of Omar. It is not to the disadvantage of the latter poet that he followed so closely in the footsteps of the earlier. A man of extraordinary genius had appeared in the world, had sung a song of incomparable beauty and power in an environment no longer worthy of him, in a language of narrow range; for many generations the song was virtually lost; then by a miracle of creation, a poet, a twin-brother in the spirit to the first, was born, who took up the forgotten poem and sang it anew with all its original melody and force, and all the accumulated refinement of ages of art. It seems to me idle to ask which was the greater master; each seems greater than his work. The song is like an instrument of precious workmanship and marvelous tone, which is worthless in common hands, but when it falls, at long intervals, into the hands of the supreme master, it yields a melody of transcendent enchantment to all that have ears to hear. If we look at the sphere of influence of the two poets, there is no longer any comparison. Omar sang to a half barbarous province; FitzGerald to the world. Wherever the English speech is spoken or read, the *Rubaiyat* have taken their place as a classic. There is not a hill-post in India, nor a village in England, where there is not a coterie to whom Omar Khayyam is a familiar friend and a bond of union. In America he has an equal following, in many regions and conditions. In the Eastern States his adepts form an esoteric sect; the beautiful volume of drawings by Mr. Vedder, is a center of delight and suggestion wherever it exists.

In the cities of the West you will find the Quatrains one of the most thoroughly read books in any club library. I heard them quoted once in one of the most lonely and desolate spots of the high Rockies. We had been camping on the Great Divide, our "roof of the world," where in the space of a few feet you may see two springs, one sending its waters to the Polar solitudes, the other to the eternal Carib summer. One morning at sunrise, as we were breaking camp, I was startled to hear one of our party, a frontiersman born, intoning these words of sombre majesty:

> 'Tis but a Tent where takes his one day's rest
> A Sultan to the realm of Death addrest;
> The Sultan rises, and the dark Ferrash
> Strikes, and prepares it for another Guest.

I thought that sublime setting of primeval forest and

pouring canyon was worthy of the lines; I am sure the dewless, crystalline air never vibrated to strains of more solemn music. Certainly, our poet can never be numbered among the great popular writers of all time. He has told no story; he has never unpacked his heart in public; he has never thrown the reins on the neck of the winged horse, and let his imagination carry him where it listed. "Ah! the crowd must have emphatic warrant," as Browning sang. Its suffrages are not for the cool, collected observer, whose eyes no glitter can dazzle, no mist suffuse. The many cannot but resent that air of lofty intelligence, that pale and subtle smile. But he will hold a place forever among that limited number who, like Lucretius and Epicurus—without rage or defiance, even without unbecoming mirth,—look deep into the tangled mysteries of things; refuse credence to the absurd, and allegiance to arrogant authority; sufficiently conscious of fallibility to be tolerant of all opinions; with a faith too wide for doctrine and a benevolence untrammeled by creed; too wise to be wholly poets, and yet too surely poets to be implacably wise.

THE RUBAIYAT

I

WAKE! For the Sun who scatter'd into flight
The Stars before him from the Field of Night,
Drives Night along with them from Heav'n, and strikes
The Sultan's Turret with a Shaft of Light.

II

BEFORE the phantom of False morning died,
Methought a Voice within the Tavern cried,
"When all the Temple is prepared within,
Why nods the drowsy Worshipper outside."

III

AND as the Cock crew, those who stood before
The Tavern shouted—"Open then the Door!
You know how little while we have to stay,
And once departed, may return no more."

IV

NOW the New Year reviving old Desires,
The thoughtful Soul to Solitude retires,
Where the White Hand of Moses on the Bough
Puts out, and Jesus from the Ground suspires.

V

IRAM indeed is gone with all his Rose,
And Jamshyd's Sev'n-ring'd Cup where no
one knows;
But still a Ruby kindles in the Vine,
And many a Garden by the Water blows.

VI

AND David's lips are lockt; but in divine
High-piping Pehlevi, with "Wine! Wine!
Wine!
Red Wine!"—the Nightingale cries to the Rose
That sallow cheek of hers to' incarnadine.

VII

COME, fill the Cup, and in the fire of Spring
Your Winter-Garment of Repentance fling:
The Bird of Time has but a little way
To flutter—and the Bird is on the Wing.

VIII

WHETHER at Naishapur or Babylon,
Whether the Cup with sweet or bitter run,
The Wine of Life keeps oozing drop by drop,
The Leaves of Life keep falling one by one.

IX

EACH Morn a thousand Roses brings, you say;
Yes, but where leaves the Rose of Yesterday?
And this first Summer month that brings the Rose
Shall take Jamshyd and Kaikobad away.

X

WELL, let it take them! What have we to do
With Kaikobad the Great, or Kaikhosru?
Let Zal and Rustum bluster as they will,
Or Hatim call to Supper—heed not you.

XI

WITH me along the strip of Herbage strown
That just divides the desert from the sown,
Where the name of Slave and Sultan is forgot—
And Peace to Mahmud on his golden Throne!

XII

A BOOK of Verses underneath the Bough,
A Jug of Wine, a Loaf of Bread—and Thou
Beside me singing in the Wilderness—
Oh, Wilderness were Paradise enow!

XIII

SOME for the Glories of This World; and some
Sigh for the Prophet's Paradise to come;
Ah, take the Cash, and let the Credit go,
Nor heed the rumble of a distant Drum!

XIV

LOOK to the blowing Rose about us—"Lo,
Laughing," she says, "into the world I blow,
At once the silken tassel of my Purse
Tear, and its Treasure on the Garden throw."

XV

AND those who husbanded the Golden grain,
And those who flung it to the winds like
Rain,
Alike to no such aureate Earth are turn'd
As, buried once, Men want dug up again.

XVI

THE Worldly Hope men set their Hearts upon
Turns Ashes—or it prospers; and anon,
Like Snow upon the Desert's dusty Face,
Lighting a little hour or two—was gone.

XVII

THINK, in this batter'd Caravanserai
Whose Portals are alternate Night and Day,
How Sultan after Sultan with his Pomp
Abode his destin'd Hour, and went his way.

XVIII

THEY say the Lion and the Lizard keep
The Courts where Jamshyd gloried and drank deep:
And Bahram, that great Hunter—the Wild Ass
Stamps o'er his Head, but cannot break his Sleep.

XIX

I SOMETIMES think that never blows so red
The Rose as where some buried Cæsar bled;
That every Hyacinth the Garden wears
Dropt in her Lap from some once lovely Head.

XX

AND this reviving Herb whose tender Green
Fledges the River-Lip on which we lean—
Ah, lean upon it lightly! for who knows
From what once lovely Lip it springs unseen!

XXI

AH, MY Beloved, fill the Cup that clears
To-day of past Regrets and future Fears:
To-morrow!—Why, To-morrow I may be
Myself with Yesterday's Sev'n thousand Years.

XXII

FOR some we loved, the loveliest and the best
That from his Vintage rolling Time hath prest,
Have drunk their Cup a Round or two before,
And one by one crept silently to rest.

XXIII

AND we, that now make merry in the Room
They left, and Summer dresses in new bloom,
Ourselves must we beneath the Couch of Earth
Descend—ourselves to make a Couch—for whom?

XXIV

AH, MAKE the most of what we yet may
spend,
Before we too into the Dust descend;
Dust into Dust, and under Dust, to lie,
Sans Wine, sans Song, sans Singer, and—sans End!

XXV

ALIKE for those who for To-day prepare,
And those that after some To-morrow stare,
A Muezzin from the Tower of Darkness cries,
"Fools! your Reward is neither Here nor There."

XXVI

WHY, all the Saints and Sages who discuss'd
Of the Two Worlds so wisely—they are thrust
Like foolish Prophets forth; their Words to Scorn
Are scatter'd, and their Mouths are stopt with Dust.

XXVII

MYSELF when young did eagerly frequent
Doctor and Saint, and heard great
argument
About it and about: but evermore
Came out by the same door where in I went.

XXVIII

WITH them the seed of Wisdom did I sow,
And with mine own hand wrought to
make it grow;
And this was all the Harvest that I reap'd—
"I came like Water, and like Wind I go."

XXIX

INTO this Universe, and Why not knowing
Nor Whence, like Water willy-nilly flowing;
And out of it, as Wind along the Waste,
I know not Whither, willy-nilly blowing.

XXX

WHAT, without asking, hither hurried
Whence?
And without asking, Whither hurried hence!
Oh, many a Cup of this forbidden Wine
Must drown the memory of that insolence!

XXXI

UP FROM Earth's Centre through the
Seventh Gate
I rose and on the Throne of Saturn sate,
And many a Knot unravel'd by the Road;
But not the Master-Knot of Human Fate.

XXXII

THERE was the Door to which I found no
Key;
There was the Veil thro' which I might not see:
Some little talk awhile of Me and Thee
There was—and then no more of Thee and Me.

XXXIII

EARTH could not answer; nor the Seas that mourn
In flowing Purple, of their Lord forlorn;
Nor rolling Heaven, with all his Signs reveal'd
And hidden by the sleeve of Night and Morn.

XXXIV

THEN of the Thee in Me who works behind
The Veil, I lifted up my hands to find
A Lamp amid the Darkness; and I heard,
As from Without—"The Me within Thee blind!"

XXXV

WHEN to the Lip of this poor earthen Urn
I lean'd, the Secret of my Life to learn:
And Lip to Lip it murmur'd—"While you live,
Drink!—for, once dead, you never shall return."

XXXVI

I THINK the Vessel, that with fugitive
Articulation answer'd, once did live,
And drink; and Ah! the passive Lip I kiss'd,
How many Kisses might it take—and give!

XXXVII

FOR I remember stopping by the way
To watch a Potter thumping his wet Clay:
And with its all-obliterated Tongue
It murmur'd—"Gently, Brother, gently, pray!"

XXXVIII

AND has not such a Story from of Old
Down Man's successive generations roll'd
Of such a clod of saturated Earth
Cast by the Maker into Human mould?

XXXIX

AND not a drop that from our Cups we
throw
For Earth to drink of, but may steal below
To quench the fire of Anguish in some Eye
There hidden—far beneath, and long ago.

XL

AS THEN the Tulip for her morning sup
Of Heav'nly Vintage from the soil
looks up,
Do you devoutly do the like, till Heav'n
To Earth invert you—like an empty Cup.

XLI

PERPLEXT no more with Human or Divine,
To-morrow's tangle to the winds resign,
And lose your fingers in the tresses of
The Cyprus-slender Minister of Wine.

XLII

AND if the Wine you drink, the Lip you press,
End in what All begins and ends in—Yes;
Think then you are To-day what Yesterday
You were—To-morrow you shall not be less.

XLIII

SO WHEN the Angel of the darker Drink
At last shall find you by the river-brink,
And offering his Cup, invite your Soul
Forth to your Lips to quaff—you shall not shrink.

XLIV

WHY, if the Soul can fling the Dust aside,
And naked on the Air of Heaven ride,
Were 't not a Shame—were 't not a Shame for him
In this clay carcase crippled to abide?

XLV

'TIS but a Tent where takes his one day's rest,
A Sultan to the realm of Death addrest;
The Sultan rises, and the dark Ferrash
Strikes, and prepares it for another Guest.

XLVI

AND fear not lest Existence closing your
Account, and mine, should know the like
no more;
The Eternal Saki from that Bowl has pour'd
Millions of Bubbles like us, and will pour.

XLVII

WHEN You and I behind the Veil are past,
Oh, but the long, long while the World shall last,
Which of our Coming and Departure heeds
As the Sea's self should heed a pebble-cast.

XLVIII

A MOMENT'S Halt—a momentary taste
Of Being from the Well amid the Waste—
And Lo!—the phantom Caravan has reacht
The Nothing it set out from—Oh, make haste!

XLIX

WOULD you that spangle of Existence
spend
About the secret—quick about it, Friend!
A Hair perhaps divides the False and True—
And upon what, prithee, does life depend?

L

A HAIR perhaps divides the False and True;
Yes; and a single Alif were the clue—
Could you but find it—to the Treasure-house,
And peradventure to The Master too;

LI

WHOSE secret Presence, through Creation's
veins
Running Quicksilver-like eludes your pains;
Taking all shapes from Mah to Mahi; and
They change and perish all—but He remains;

LII

A MOMENT guess'd—then back behind
the Fold
Immerst of Darkness round the Drama roll'd
Which, for the Pastime of Eternity,
He doth Himself contrive, enact, behold.

LIII

BUT if in vain, down on the stubborn floor
Of Earth, and up to Heav'n's unopening
Door,
You gaze To-day, while You are You—how then
To-morrow, when You shall be You no more?

LIV

WASTE not your Hour, nor in the vain
pursuit
Of This and That endeavour and dispute;
Better be jocund with the fruitful Grape
Than sadden after none, or bitter, Fruit.

LV

YOU know, my Friends, with what a brave
Carouse
I made a Second Marriage in my house;
Divorced old barren Reason from my Bed,
And took the Daughter of the Vine to Spouse.

LVI

FOR "Is" and "Is-not" though with Rule
and Line,
And "Up-and-down" by Logic I define,
Of all that one should care to fathom, I
Was never deep in anything but—Wine.

LVII

AH, BUT my Computations, People say,
Reduced the Year to better reckoning?—
Nay,
'Twas only striking from the Calendar
Unborn To-morrow, and dead Yesterday.

LVIII

AND lately by the Tavern Door agape,
Came shining through the Dusk an Angel
Shape
Bearing a Vessel on his Shoulder; and
He bid me taste of it; and 't was—the Grape!

LIX

THE Grape that can with Logic absolute
The Two-and-Seventy jarring Sects confute:
The sovereign Alchemist that in a trice
Life's leaden metal into Gold transmute:

LX

THE mighty Mahmud, Allah-breathing Lord,
That all the misbelieving and black Horde
Of Fears and Sorrows that infest the Soul
Scatters before him with his whirlwind Sword.

LXI

WHY, be this Juice the growth of God, who dare
Blaspheme the twisted tendril as a Snare?
A Blessing, we should use it, should we not?
And if a Curse—why, then, Who set it there?

LXII

I MUST abjure the Balm of Life, I must,
Scared by some After-reckoning ta'en on trust,
Or lured with Hope of some Diviner Drink,
To fill the Cup—when crumbled into Dust!

LXIII

O THREATS of Hell and Hopes of Paradise!
One thing at least is certain—This Life flies;
One thing is certain and the rest is Lies;
The Flower that once has blown for ever dies.

LXIV

STRANGE, is it not? that of the myriads who
Before us pass'd the door of Darkness through,
Not one returns to tell us of the Road,
Which to discover we must travel too.

LXV

THE Revelations of Devout and Learn'd
Who rose before us, and as Prophets burn'd,
Are all but Stories, which, awoke from Sleep
They told their comrades, and to Sleep return'd.

LXVI

I SENT my Soul through the Invisible,
Some letter of that After-life to spell;
And by and by my Soul return'd to me,
And answer'd "I Myself am Heav'n and Hell:"

LXVII

HEAV'N but the Vision of fulfill'd Desire,
And Hell the Shadow from a Soul on fire
Cast on the Darkness into which Ourselves,
So late emerg'd from, shall so soon expire.

LXVIII

WE ARE no other than a moving row
Of Magic Shadow-shapes that come and go
Round with the Sun-illumin'd Lantern held
In Midnight by the Master of the Show;

LXIX

BUT helpless Pieces of the Game He plays
Upon this Chequer-board of Nights and Days;
Hither and thither moves, and checks, and slays,
And one by one back in the Closet lays.

LXX

THE Ball no question makes of Ayes and Noes,
But Here or There as strikes the Player goes;
And He that toss'd you down into the Field,
He knows about it all—He knows—He knows!

LXXI

THE Moving Finger writes; and having writ,
Moves on: nor all your Piety nor Wit
Shall lure it back to cancel half a Line,
Nor all your Tears wash out a Word of it.

LXXII

AND that inverted Bowl they call the Sky,
Whereunder crawling coop'd we live and die,
Lift not your hands to It for help—for It
As impotently moves as you or I.

LXXIII

WITH Earth's first Clay They did the Last
Man knead,
And there of the Last Harvest sow'd the Seed:
And the first Morning of Creation wrote
What the Last Dawn of Reckoning shall read.

LXXIV

YESTERDAY This Day's Madness did
prepare;
To-Morrow's Silence, Triumph, or Despair:
Drink! for you know not whence you came, nor why:
Drink! for you know not why you go, nor where.

LXXV

I TELL you this—When, started from the
Goal,
Over the flaming shoulders of the Foal
Of Heav'n Parwin and Mushtari they flung,
In my predestin'd Plot of Dust and Soul.

LXXVI

THE Vine had struck a fibre: which about
If clings my Being—let the Dervish flout;
Of my Base metal may be filed a Key,
That shall unlock the Door he howls without.

LXXVII

AND this I know: whether the one True
Light
Kindle to Love, or Wrath consume me quite,
One Flash of It within the Tavern caught
Better than in the Temple lost outright.

LXXVIII

WHAT! out of senseless Nothing to provoke
A conscious Something to resent the
yoke
Of unpermitted Pleasure, under pain
Of Everlasting Penalties, if broke!

LXXIX

WHAT! from his helpless Creature be repaid
Pure Gold for what he lent him dross-allay'd—
Sue for a Debt we never did contract,
And cannot answer—Oh the sorry trade!

LXXX

O THOU, who didst with pitfall and with gin
Beset the Road I was to wander in,
Thou wilt not with Predestin'd Evil round
Enmesh, and then impute my Fall to Sin!

LXXXI

OH THOU, who Man of baser Earth didst make,
And ev'n with Paradise devise the Snake:
For all the Sin wherewith the Face of Man
Is blacken'd—Man's forgiveness give—and take!

LXXXII

AS UNDER cover of departing Day
Slunk hunger-stricken Ramazan away,
Once more within the Potter's house alone
I stood, surrounded by the Shapes of Clay.

LXXXIII

SHAPES of all Sorts and Sizes, great and
small,
That stood along the floor and by the wall;
And some loquacious Vessels were; and some
Listen'd perhaps, but never talk'd at all.

LXXXIV

SAID one among them—"Surely not in vain
My substance of the common Earth was ta'en
And to this Figure moulded, to be broke,
Or trampled back to shapeless Earth again."

LXXXV

THEN said a Second—"Ne'er a peevish Boy
Would break the Bowl from which he drank in joy;
And He that with His hand the Vessel made
Will surely not in after Wrath destroy."

LXXXVI

AFTER a momentary silence spake
Some Vessel of a more ungainly Make;
"They sneer at me for leaning all awry:
What! did the Hand then of the Potter shake?"

LXXXVII

WHEREAT some one of the loquacious
Lot—
I think a Sufi pipkin—waxing hot—
"All this of Pot and Potter—Tell me then,
Who is the Potter, pray, and who the Pot?"

LXXXVIII

WHY," said another, "Some there are who
tell
Of one who threatens he will toss to Hell
The luckless Pots he marr'd in making—Pish!
He's a Good Fellow, and 't will all be well."

LXXXIX

"WELL," murmur'd one, "Let whoso make
or buy,
My Clay with long Oblivion is gone dry:
But fill me with the old familiar Juice,
Methinks I might recover by and by."

XC

SO WHILE the Vessels one by one were
speaking,
The little Moon look'd in all that were seeking:
And then they jogg'd each other, "Brother! Brother!
Now for the Porter's shoulder-knot a-creaking!"

XCI

AH, WITH the Grape my fading Life provide,
And wash the Body whence the Life has died,
And lay me, shrouded in the living Leaf,
By some not unfrequented Garden-side.

XCII

THAT ev'n my buried Ashes such a snare
Of Vintage shall fling up into the Air
As not a True-believer passing by
But shall be overtaken unaware.

XCIII

INDEED the Idols I have loved so long
Have done my credit in this World much wrong:
Have drown'd my Glory in a shallow Cup,
And sold my Reputation for a Song.

XCIV

INDEED, indeed, Repentance oft before
I swore—but was I sober when I swore?
And then and then came Spring, and Rose-in-hand
My thread-bare Penitence apieces tore.

XCV

AND much as Wine has play'd the Infidel,
And robb'd me of my Robe of Honour—
Well,
I wonder often what the Vintners buy
One half so precious as the stuff they sell.

XCVI

YET Ah, that Spring should vanish with the
Rose!
That Youth's sweet-scented manuscript should close!
The Nightingale that in the branches sang,
Ah whence and whither flown again, who knows!

XCVII

WOULD but the Desert of the Fountain yield
One glimpse—if dimly, yet indeed, reveal'd,
  To which the fainting Traveller might spring,
As springs the trampled herbage of the field!

XCVIII

WOULD but some winged Angel ere too late
Arrest the yet unfolded Roll of Fate,
  And make the stern Recorder otherwise
Enregister, or quite obliterate!

XCIX

AH LOVE! could you and I with Him
conspire
To grasp this sorry Scheme of Things entire,
Would not we shatter it to bits—and then
Re-mould it nearer to the Heart's Desire!

C

YON rising Moon that looks for us again—
How oft hereafter will she wax and wane;
How oft hereafter rising look for us
Through this same Garden—and for one in vain!

CI

AND when like her, oh Saki, you shall pass
Among the Guests Star-scatter'd on the Grass,
And in your joyous errand reach the spot
Where I made One—turn down an empty Glass!

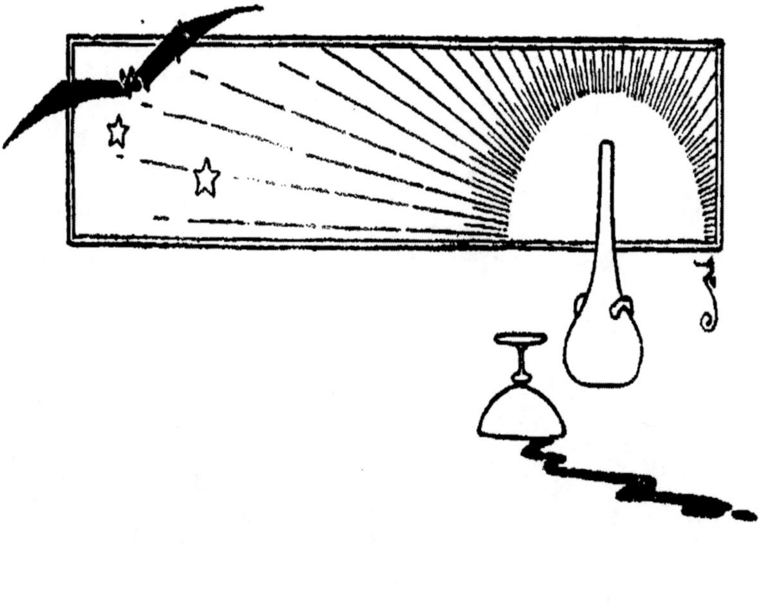

SO HERE ENDETH *THE RUBAIYAT* OF OMAR KHAYYAM, AS TRANSLATED INTO ENGLISH BY EDWARD FITZGERALD AND DONE INTO A PRINTED BOOK BY THE ROYCROFTERS, AT THEIR SHOP IN EAST AURORA, WHICH IS IN ERIE COUNTY, NEW YORK, IN APRIL, MCMVI

ROYCROFT